SUMMER SMARTS

Activities and Skills to Prepare Students for 1st Grade

Jeanne Crane Castafero and Janet van Roden

Houghton Mifflin Company
New Ways to Know®

Dear Parents:

What is the purpose of Summer Smarts?

Summer Smarts is a unique integration of material to help your kindergartner get ready for first grade. *Summer Smarts* contains worksheets to review various skills and suggests books to read to develop children's language skills.

What kind of kindergartner can use Summer Smarts?

In our research, it became apparent that expectations for kindergartners vary not just from state to state, but from one school district to the next. Consequently, we have created a book that can be used by kindergartners at many levels.

Does it matter if my kindergartner is not yet a reader?

Besides agreeing that kindergartners should be able to identify letters by name, there is little agreement about which skills should be mastered in kindergarten. Most kindergartens do not teach reading *per se*. We have considered this fact, while recognizing that many kindergartners do indeed finish kindergarten not just with the ability to recognize sight words but also with substantial decoding skills. This book has value for both readers and nonreaders. Nonreaders will require more parental involvement; readers will have ample opportunity to practice decoding skills.

How well must my child write and spell in order to do Summer Smarts?

Spelling is a developmental process. It happens over time with good coaching, just like learning to talk. Some kindergartners will be able to spell a core group of words. Other children will write the letters that they hear, which, because the English language is not entirely predictable, are not necessarily all the letters in a word. For example, a child might write "I pla bsktbl" for "I play basketball." Such spelling tells you that the child has a good grasp of consonants but needs to learn about vowels.

Encourage your child to stretch words out to listen for all the sounds. Help your child learn words that he or she uses a lot; for example, *mom, dad, and, I,* and *love.* Above all, avoid frustration. Take dictation if the words your child wants to use are beyond his or her writing vocabulary.

How should Summer Smarts be used?

Though some children will be able to read the simple instructions and paragraphs in this book, *Summer Smarts* is not intended for independent use by most kindergarten graduates. Some sections, which will vary by child, require an adult's assistance. Help children go beyond the pages, too. Read not only the poems and rhymes in *Summer Smarts*, but also other poems and rhymes. Count or measure not only the items in *Summer Smarts*, count and measure things everywhere.

Reading aloud to children is very important. We have recommended books to read in the Read About It feature at the bottom of selected pages. In addition, the Book Section includes worksheets for specific books. For the most part, we expect the reading and worksheets to be done with an adult.

We hope that you and your child enjoy *Summer Smarts!* Use discretion about the pace at which you use this book and even about how much of the workbook your child completes. There is an answer key at the end to assist you and your child. Have a great—and smart—summer.

Sincerely,

Jeanne   *Janet*

Jeanne Crane Castafero and Janet van Roden

Contents

1 **Who Am I?**   General knowledge

2 **Where Do I Live?**   Address, telephone number

3 **Aa**   Letter formation and sound

4 **All Aboard!**   Number formation

6 **Always Adding**   Addition

7 **Bb**   Letter formation and sound

8 **Belle at the Beach**   Initial consonants

9 **Beautiful Babies**   Matching

10 **Cc**   Letter formation and sound

11 **Crazy Compounds**   Compound words

12 **Castle Calendar**   Reading a calendar

14 **Dd**   Letter formation and sound

15 **Dandy Drawing**   Drawing

16 **Do the Days**   Days of the week

17 **Ee**   Letter formation and sound

18 **Eggs, Eggs**   Number, color, and rhyming words; subtraction

20 **Easy Experiment**   Science

22 **Ff**   Letter formation and sound

23 **Flower Facts**   Addition, subtraction, counting

24 Fun Friends   Writing, drawing

25 Gg   Letter formation and sound

26 Goldilocks and Friends   Nursery rhymes, fairy tales

27 Goofy Gus   Patterns

28 Hh   Letter formation and sound

29 Happy Holidays   Counting

30 Hannah's House   Map reading

31 Ii   Letter formation and sound

32 Inch by Inch   Measuring

33 Jj   Letter formation and sound

34 Jam and Jug   Rhyming words, phonograms

35 Jiggle Jaggle   Following directions, colors

36 Kk   Letter formation and sound

37 Kings and Keys   Science

38 Ll   Letter formation and sound

39 Lincoln's Life   History, listening comprehension

41 Line Lesson   Ordinal numbers

42 Mm   Letter formation and sound

43 Mish Mash   General knowledge

44 Nn   Letter formation and sound

45 Ned's Newsstand   Money

47 Nice Numbers   Counting, writing numbers, adding

49 Oo   Letter formation and sound

50 Only Opposites   Opposites, high-frequency words

51 Out! Out!   Classification

52 Pp   Letter formation and sound

53 Pretty Patterns   Patterns

54 Peter, Peter, Pumpkin Eater   Consonants, rhyming words

55 Qq   Letter formation and sound

56 Quote Questions   Listening comprehension

57 Rr   Letter formation and sound

58 Rescue Robby   Following directions

59 Ready to Rhyme   Rhyming words, phonograms, consonants

61 Ss   Letter formation and sound

62 Sam's Senses   The five senses

63 Special Seasons   Seasons

64 Tt   Letter formation and sound

65 Teddy Bear, Teddy Bear   Consonants, rhythm, rhyme

66 Telling Time   Time to the hour and half hour

67 Uu   Letter formation and sound

68 Under the Umbrella   Short vowels

69 United Under the Flag   History, listening comprehension

71 Vv   Letter formation and sound

72 Very Victor   Initial consonants

73 Vowels   Long vowels

74 Ww   Letter formation and sound

75 What Do You See?   Observing, writing

76 Wonderful World   Geography

77 Xx   Letter formation and sound

78 X It!   Safety rules

79 Yy   Letter formation and sound

80 Your Yardstick   Measuring

81 Zz   Letter formation and sound

82 Zany Zoo   Addition, subtraction, word problems

83 Zzzz...   Writing

BOOK SECTION

85 *No More Water in the Tub!* by Tedd Arnold

87 *Hattie and the Fox* by Mem Fox

88 *The Napping House* by Audrey Wood

89 Answer Key

Who Am I?

_____
- -

My name is _____.

Complete the sentences.
Color the pictures.

_____
- -

My eyes are _____.

_____
- -

My hair is _____.

_____
- -

My favorite color is _____.

Here is a picture of my family.

Where Do I Live?

Your address and telephone number are important.
Write your address and telephone number
on the lines below.

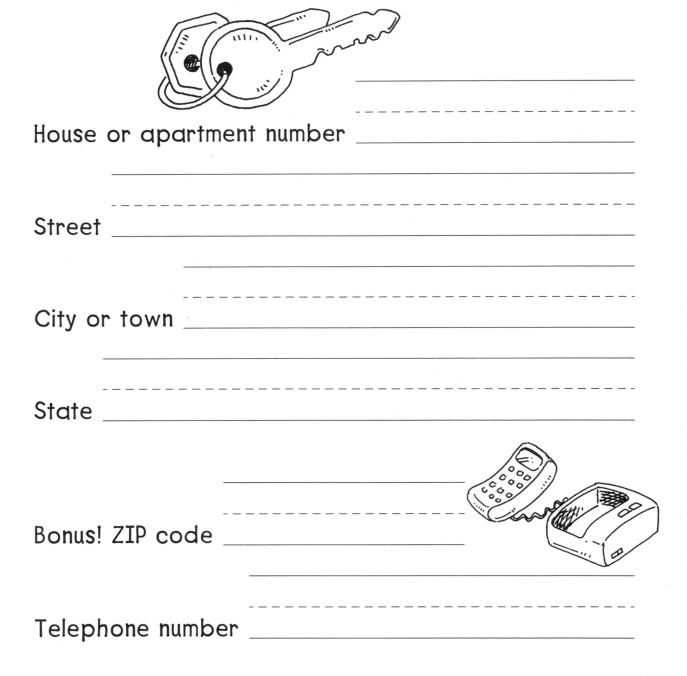

House or apartment number _____

Street _____

City or town _____

State _____

Bonus! ZIP code _____

Telephone number _____

Aa

Annie the alligator has an apple.

Circle all the **a**'s in the sentence about Annie.
Then write each uppercase and lowercase
letter six times.

A

a

Draw something that begins with the letter **a**.
Write the word.

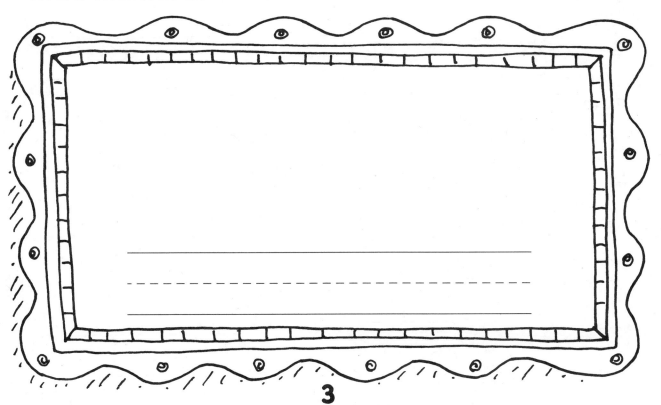

All Aboard!

Fill each boxcar with the **number** in the engine.

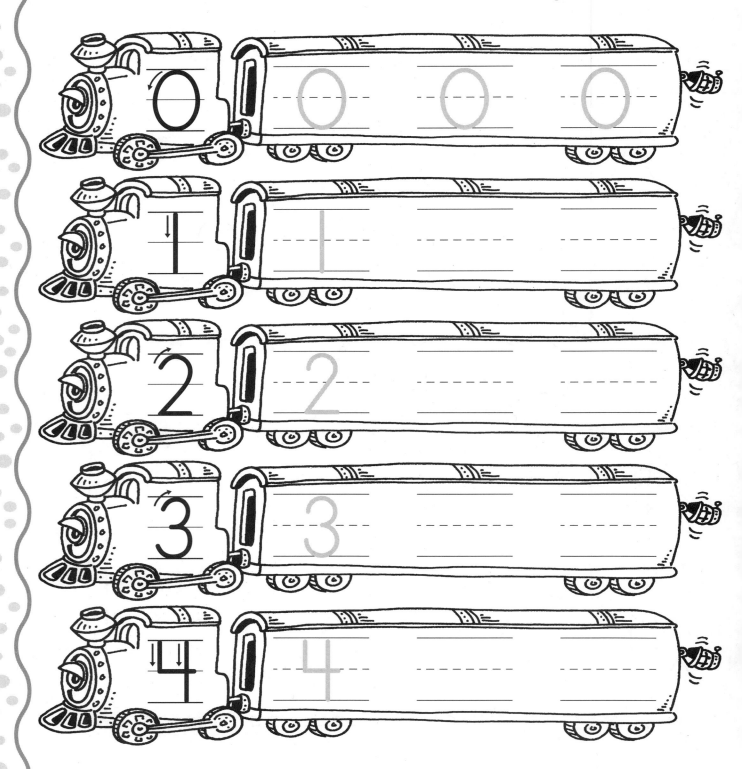

 **Read About It**

Read *Count the Animals 1 2 3*
by Demi for a fun book about counting.

5

Always Adding

Fill in the number sentences.
The first one is done for you.

1.

   2 + 3 = 5 apples

2.

   ____ + ____ = ____ airplanes

3.

   ____ + ____ = ____ ants

4.

   ____ + ____ = ____ arrows

Bobby the balloon is over a boat.

Write each uppercase and
lowercase letter six times.

B

b

Draw something that begins with the letter **b**.
Write the word on the line.

Belle at the Beach

Circle all the things in the picture that begin with <u>b</u>.

Beautiful Babies

The Turtle

A big turtle sat on the end of a log.
Watching a tadpole turn into a frog.

Anonymous

Draw a line from the animal to its baby.

1.

A.

2.

B.

3.

C.

4.

D.

5.

E.

Read
About It

Read *Is Your Mama a Llama?*
by Deborah Guarino.
Whose mama is a llama?

Cc

Carol the canary is in the cage.

Write each uppercase and lowercase letter six times.

C

c

Draw something that begins with the letter <u>c</u>. Write the word.

Crazy Compounds

A compound word is one word made up of two smaller words, like **baseball**.

Draw a line from the words on the left to the words on the right to make compound words.

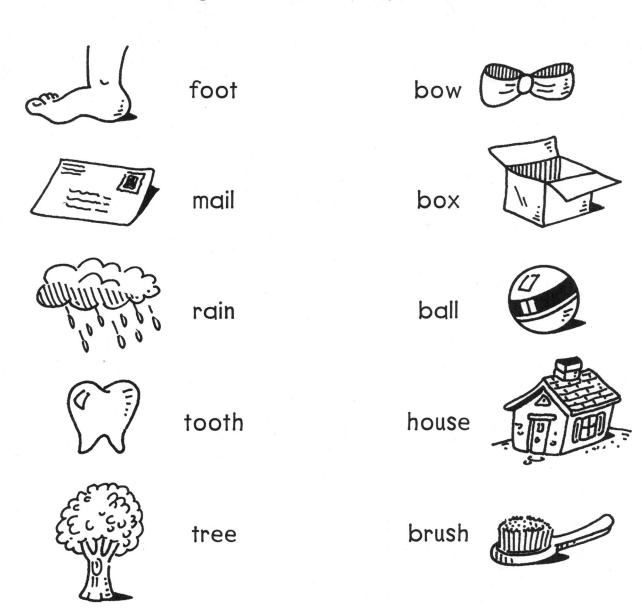

foot

mail

rain

tooth

tree

bow

box

ball

house

brush

Castle Calendar

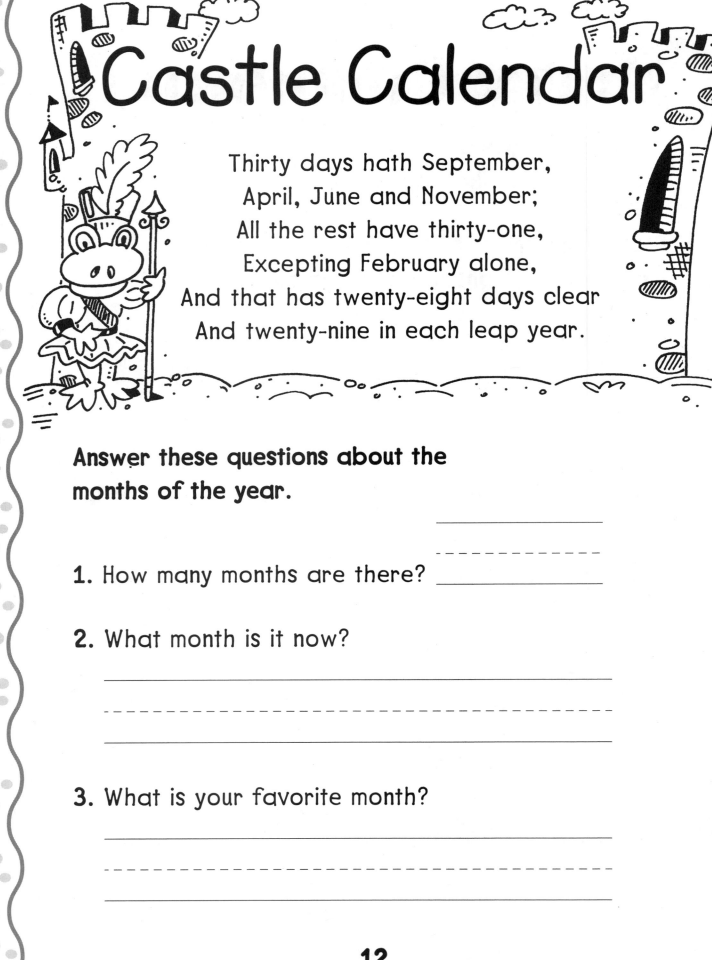

Thirty days hath September,
April, June and November;
All the rest have thirty-one,
Excepting February alone,
And that has twenty-eight days clear
And twenty-nine in each leap year.

Answer these questions about the months of the year.

1. How many months are there? _____

2. What month is it now?

_____

_____

_____

3. What is your favorite month?

_____

_____

_____

June

Sunday	Monday	Tuesday	Wednesday	Thursday	Friday	Saturday
				1	2	3
4	5	6	7	8	9	10
11	12	13	14	15	16	17
18	19	20	21	22	23	24
25	26	27	28	29	30	

1. Draw a star next to the word June.

2. Circle the names of the days of the week.

_____

- - - - - - - -

3. How many days are in a week? _____

_____

- - - - - - - - - - - -

4. How many days are in June? _____

Read About It

Read *Today Is Monday* by Eric Carle. What do you like to eat on Monday?

Dd

Danny the dragon is dancing.

Write each uppercase and lowercase letter six times.

D

d

Draw something that begins with the letter **d**.
Write the word.

14

Dandy Drawing

Draw something that makes you laugh.

Draw something that makes you think of summer.

Draw something that you love to eat.

Draw something that you can do yourself.

Do the Days

Write the days in order in the boxes.

Tuesday

Sunday

Thursday

Friday

Saturday

Monday

Wednesday

1. Sunday

2.

3.

4.

5.

6.

7.

Ee

Ellie the elephant is exercising.

Write each uppercase and lowercase letter six times.

E

e

Draw something that begins with the letter **e**.
Write the word.

Eggs, Eggs

Chook, chook, chook, chook, chook
Good morning, Mrs. Hen.
How many chickens have you got?
Madam, I've got ten.
Four of them are yellow,
And four of them are brown,
And two of them are speckled red,
The nicest in the town.

Anonymous

1. Circle the number words.

2. Circle each color word with the matching crayon.

_____

- - - - - - - - - - - - - - - - - - -

3. What word rhymes with **hen**? _____

_____

- - - - - - - - - - - - - - - - - - -

4. What word rhymes with **brown**? _____

Let's do some subtraction.
The first one is done for you.

1. 5 - 3 = __2__

2. 4 - 2 = _____

3. 6 - 3 = _____

4. 5 - 1 = _____

5. 3 - 2 = _____

 **Read About It** For a book about chickens, read *Chicken Little* as retold and illustrated by Steven Kellogg.

19

Easy Experiment

Do this with an adult.

What you will need
- two jars filled with water
- white construction paper
- black construction paper
- sunny day or a bright lamp

Instructions

1. Completely cover one jar with the white paper.

2. Completely cover the other jar with the black paper.

3. Put both jars in a very sunny place or directly under the lamp. Let them sit for several hours.

4. After the time has passed, use your hand or finger to feel the water in each jar.

What did you find out? Circle the correct answer.

1. The water in which jar was hotter?
   a. the water in the jar covered with white paper

   b. the water in the jar covered with black paper

Dark colors like black take in more heat from the sun than light colors.

2. On a sunny summer day, what color shirt do you think would make you hotter?
   a black shirt   a white shirt

3. If you were in the desert, what color clothes would you wear to be cooler?
   black   white

Ff

Fred the frog is on the fence.

Write each uppercase and
lowercase letter six times.

F

f

Draw something that begins with the letter **f**.
Write the word.

Flower Facts

Fill in a plus or minus in each circle.

1. 1 ⊕ 2 = 3

2. 3 ◯ 4 = 7

3. 5 ◯ 3 = 2

4. 5 ◯ 5 = 0

5. 3 ◯ 3 = 6

6. 3 ◯ 3 = 0

7. 4 ◯ 2 = 6

8. 4 ◯ 4 = 8

9. 3 ◯ 1 = 2

10. 5 ◯ 1 = 4

Draw in the missing flowers so each pot has six flowers.

Fun Friends

It is so much fun to have good friends!
Who is your best friend? Draw a picture
of your friend. Then write about your friend.

_____

- -

_____

- -

_____

 **Read About It**

Read *My Best Friend* by Pat Hutchins
for a great story about best friends.
Why are the two children in the story
good friends?

Gg

Gail the goose is in the garden.

Write each uppercase and
lowercase letter six times.

G

g

Draw something that begins with the letter **g**.
Write the word.

Goldilocks and Friends

Circle the answers.

1. Little Bo-Peep lost her _____.
   cow   sheep
   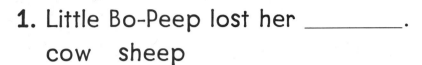

2. Little Miss Muffet sat on a _____.
   chair   tuffet

3. Jack Sprat could eat no _____.
   fat   corn

4. Old King Cole was a merry old _____.
   man   soul

5. _____ ate the bears' porridge.
   Gretel   Goldilocks

6. Little Red Riding Hood visited her _____.
   grandmother   wolf

7. There were _____ little pigs.
   three   four

8. Jack grew a giant _____.
   cornstalk   beanstalk

Goofy Gus

Here are two boxes with different patterns.
Finish the last row of each pattern.

Make up your own pattern using colors or shapes.

Hh

Harry the horse has a hat.

Write each uppercase and lowercase letter six times.

Draw something that begins with the letter **h**.
Write the word.

Happy Holidays

Count the number of holiday things in each box.
Write the number next to the box.

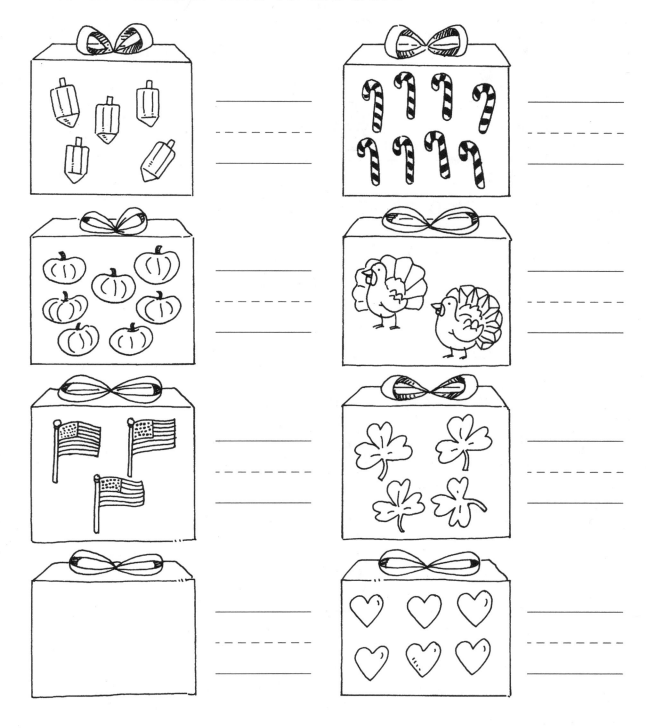

Hannah's House

Look at the map of Hannah's room.

1. Draw a line under the two sentences that are true.

- The bed is east of the chest.

- The toybox is north of the lamp.

- The bed is west of the chest.

- The lamp is north of the toybox.

Fill in the blank.

2. The chest is _____ of the bed.

3. The toybox is _____ of the lamp.

I i

Ida the iguana is on the igloo.

Write each uppercase and lowercase letter six times.

I

i

Draw something that begins with the letter **i**.
Write the word.

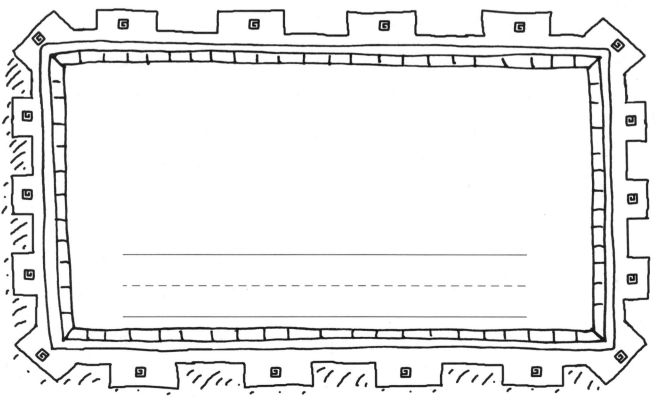

Inch by Inch

Use a ruler to measure the lines.
Write the number of inches.

1. _____ inch

2. _____ inches

3. _____ inches

Find some things of your own to measure, like a book or your finger. Write them here.

What I measured   How many inches

_____

_____

_____

0	1	2	3	4	5	6

Jj

Jerry the jaguar eats jelly from a jar.

Write each uppercase and
lowercase letter six times.

Draw something that begins with the letter **j**.
Write the word.

Jam and Jug

Write the words that rhyme with <u>jam</u>.

_____

1. a boy's name _____

_____

2. a girl's name _____

_____

3. something to eat with eggs _____

Write the words that rhyme with <u>jug</u>.

_____

4. something you do with your arms _____

_____

5. an insect _____

_____

6. a floor covering _____

Make up a tongue twister with as many <u>j</u> words as you can. Here's one: Jimmy Joe jumps joyfully.

34

Jiggle Jaggle

Draw a funny jiggle jaggle picture.

Draw an orange tree with purple leaves.

Draw blue grass.

Draw a green cat with a red hat sitting under the tree.

Kelly the kangaroo is flying a kite.

Write each uppercase and lowercase letter six times.

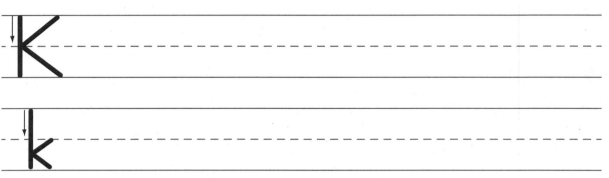

K

k

Draw something that begins with the letter **k**. Write the word.

36

Kings and Keys

Circle the objects that you can roll.
Cross out the objects that you cannot roll.

Draw something that rolls.	Draw something that does not roll.

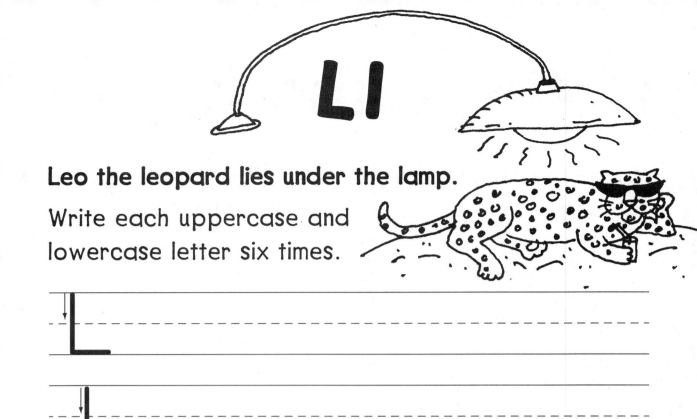

Ll

Leo the leopard lies under the lamp.

Write each uppercase and lowercase letter six times.

Draw something that begins with the letter **l**.
Write the word.

Lincoln's Life

Have an adult read this to you.

Abraham Lincoln was our country's sixteenth president. He was born in a one-room log cabin in Kentucky on February 12, 1809. Abraham and his family lived on a farm where he and his sister Sarah worked hard helping out with the chores. When they had time, they walked two miles to a log school house.

When Abraham was seven, his family moved west to the wilderness of Indiana. Land had to be cleared for a new farm. Young Abraham was big and very strong for his age. He helped his father clear the land by cutting down trees with his ax.

There were not many schools in the wilderness so Abraham did not go to school often. But he was a hard worker, and he taught himself to read and write.

When Abraham was not busy with chores, he loved to read books, often reading into the night by the light of the fire. Books were hard to come by in the wilderness, but Abraham read every book he could get his hands on. Sometimes, he walked as many as twenty miles to borrow a book.

Abraham left home when he was twenty-one years old. He moved to Illinois. At first, he worked in a general store. Once he charged a woman six and a quarter cents too much. When he discovered his mistake, he walked three miles to pay her back. People started calling him "Honest Abe."

Talk about these questions with an adult.

1. Abraham Lincoln was the sixteenth president of the United States. Who was the first president? Who is the president now?

2. Did Abraham Lincoln grow up in the country or a city? How do you know?

3. How did Abraham Lincoln learn to read and write?

4. Why did people call Abraham Lincoln "Honest Abe"?

Draw a picture of young Abraham.

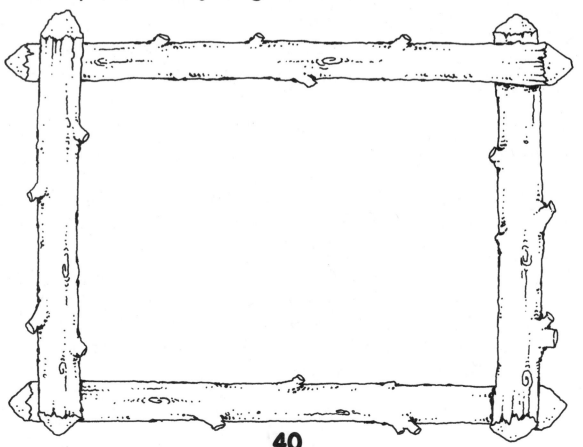

40

Line Lesson

Tell the place of each animal in the line.

first
second
third
fourth
fifth

_____

1. The lion is _____ in line.

_____

2. The elephant is _____ in line.

_____

3. The snake is _____ in line.

_____

4. The giraffe is _____ in line.

_____

5. The monkey is _____ in line.

41

Mm

Meg the mouse is on the moon.

Write each uppercase and lowercase letter six times.

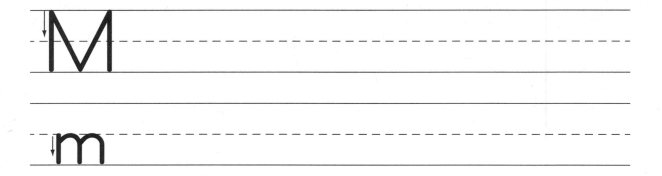

M

m

Draw something that begins with the letter **m**.
Write the word.

Mish Mash

Circle the answer.

1. the color of an apple   orange   red

2. the opposite of **big**   good   little

3. a shape with 3 sides   square   triangle

4. the number after 8   7   9

5. the number of pennies
   in a nickel   ten   five

6. the number that
   comes before 3   1   2

7. the box in the middle   ■   ■   ■

8. a word that rhymes with **pat**   fan   fat

9. the number of fingers you have   five   ten

10. the biggest triangle   ▲   ▲   ▲

Nn

Ned the newt is reading the news.

Write each uppercase and
lowercase letter six times.

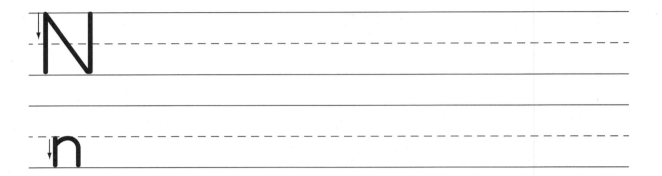

N

n

Draw something that begins with the letter **n**.
Write the word.

Ned's Newsstand

Match the objects to the coins that show how much they cost.

1.

A.

2.

B.

3.

C.

4.

D.

Color in the number of coins you need.

Write the number of pennies.

46

Nice Numbers

Write how many.

1. letters in your first name _____

2. letters in your last name _____

3. teeth in your mouth _____

4. bathrooms at home _____

5. TV sets at home _____

6. doors at home _____

7. pets at home _____

8. Which number is the highest? _____

Now add these numbers. You may use counters.

9. 2 + 3 = _____   13. 5 + 0 = _____

10. 1 + 4 = _____   14. 6 + 0 = _____

11. 2 + 2 = _____   15. 3 + 3 = _____

12. 3 + 1 = _____   16. 4 + 2 = _____

Oo

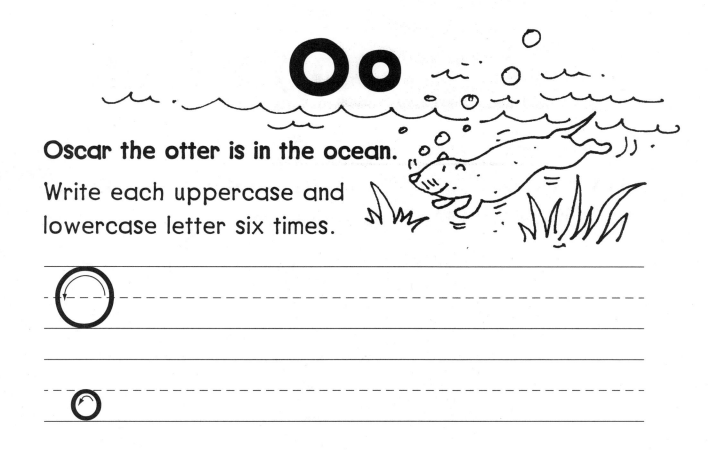

Oscar the otter is in the ocean.

Write each uppercase and
lowercase letter six times.

Draw something that begins with the letter **o**.
Write the word.

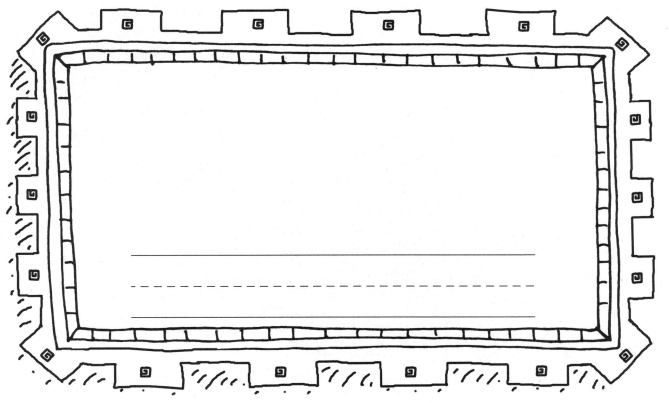

Only Opposites

Look at each word.
Find a word in the sign that means the opposite.
Write it on the line.

big   no
go
on   in

1. out _____

2. stop _____

3. little _____

4. off _____

5. yes _____

50

Out! Out!

In each row, cross out the picture that does not belong. Color the pictures in each row that do belong.

soccer ball   baseball   bat   basketball

mitten   swimsuit   ski hat   scarf

hamburger   apple   banana   grapes

book   pencil   ruler   skates

elephant   tiger   bird   giraffe

Pp

Peter the panther is painting pictures.

Write each uppercase and lowercase letter six times.

P

p

Draw something that begins with the letter **p**. Write the word.

Pretty Patterns

Look at the shapes. Do you see the pattern?
Complete each pattern by drawing
the shapes that come next.

1.  ___ ___

2.  ___ ___ ___ ___

3.  ___ ___ ___

4.  ___ ___ ___

Draw your own pattern.

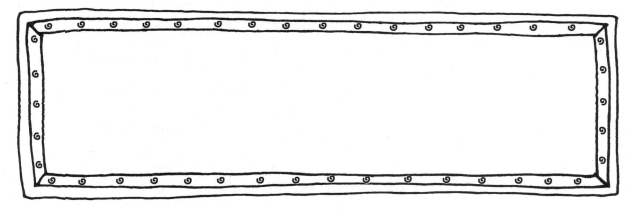

53

Peter, Peter, Pumpkin Eater

Read the nursery rhyme.

Peter, Peter, pumpkin eater,
Had a wife and couldn't keep her;
He put her in a pumpkin shell
And there he kept her very well.

1. Circle all the **p**'s in the rhyme.
How many are there?

_____

- - - - - - - - - - - - - - -

_____

2. Draw a line under two words that rhyme.

3. Write some more words that rhyme with **well**.

_____

- -

_____

4. Write some more words that begin with **p**.

_____

- -

_____

Qq

Quentin the quail is under the quilt.

Write each uppercase and
lowercase letter six times.

Q

q

Draw something that begins with the letter **q**.
Write the word.

Quote Questions

Read this page with an adult.

1. A watched pot never boils.

Jenny was waiting for her friend to pick her up to go to the movies. She sat staring out the window, hoping that each car she saw would be her friend's. Jenny's mom shook her head and said, "Jenny, a watched pot never boils."

What do you think she meant?

2. The early bird catches the worm.

Peter loved the chocolate doughnuts with sprinkles that the bakery made. The problem was that lots of other kids did, too. Peter was often disappointed to find that the doughnuts were all gone when he got to the bakery. One morning, Peter set his alarm clock so he could get to the bakery before the other kids. As he raced out the door, Peter heard his mom call to him, "The early bird catches the worm!"

What do you think his mother meant?

Rr

Rusty the rooster is on the roof.

Write each uppercase and lowercase letter six times.

R

r

Draw something that begins with the letter **r**.
Write the word.

Rescue Robby

Robby is stuck in the tree! Build a ladder of shapes to rescue him. As you plan the size of your shapes, make sure that the ladder is not too short and not too tall. Build it as follows:

1. Draw one red rectangle ▭ on the ground.

2. On top of the red rectangle ▭, draw 2 green circles ○ ○.

3. On top of the circles ○ ○, draw 3 blue triangles △△△.

4. On the very top, draw 1 orange square □.

Now you should be able to rescue Robby!

Why might Robby have run up into the tree?

_____

- -

_____

Ready to Rhyme

Write a word that rhymes with the picture.
Draw a picture of the rhyming word.

pocket ___r___ocket   tail _____ail

rug _____ug   car _____ar

spoon _____oon   tree _____ee

Circle the rhyming words in each line.

1. belly   bank   smelly   smoke

2. done   dish   dark   fish

3. spin   farm   face   space

4. house   mouse   mice   home

Circle the pictures in each row that rhyme.

5.

6.

7.

Read About It For a fun book that uses rhyme, read *Sheep in a Jeep* by Nancy Shaw. Can you find five words in it that rhyme with *sheep*?

60

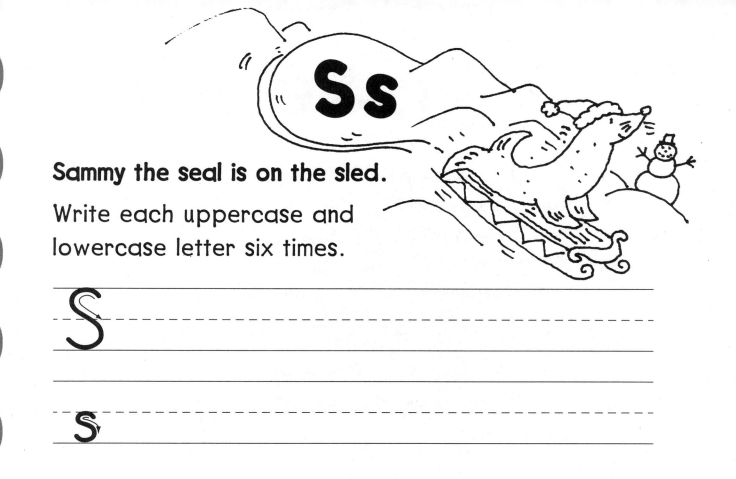

Ss

Sammy the seal is on the sled.

Write each uppercase and lowercase letter six times.

S

s

Draw something that begins with the letter <u>s</u>. Write the word.

Sam's Senses

There are five senses that we use
to explore our world.

See   Hear   Taste   Touch   Smell

**Under each picture, write the sense
that Sam is using.**

Special Seasons

There are four seasons in a year:
spring, summer, fall, and winter.

Draw a ✿ in the box above the spring words.
Draw a ✿ in the box above the summer words.
Draw a 🍂 in the box above the fall words.
Draw a ⛄ in the box above the winter words.

falling leaves
football games
Halloween

corn on the cob
Fourth of July
summer vacation

baby animals
daffodils
spring showers

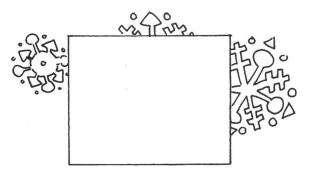

snowflakes
shorter days
mittens

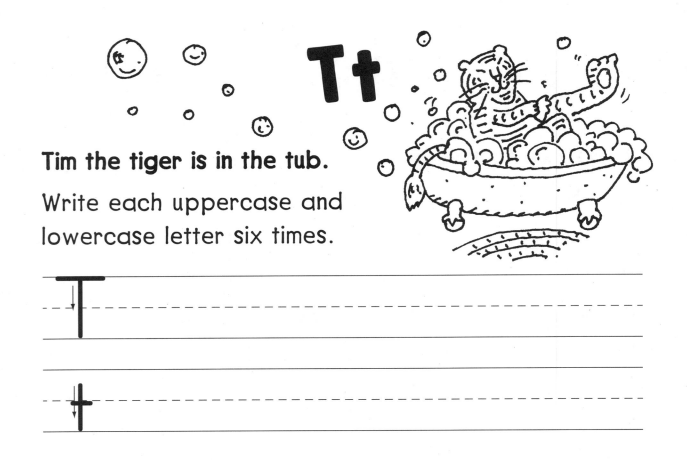

T t

Tim the tiger is in the tub.

Write each uppercase and lowercase letter six times.

Draw something that begins with the letter **t**.
Write the word.

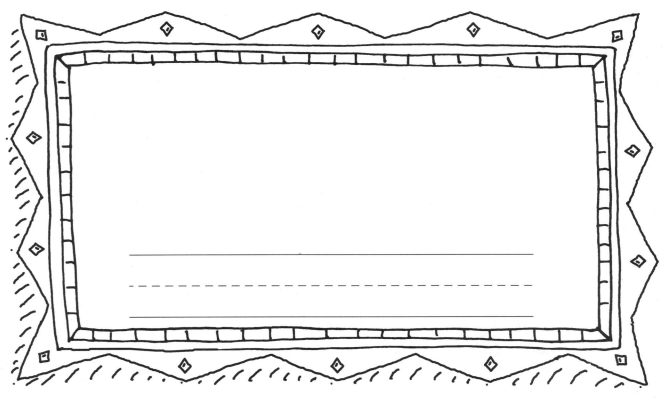

Teddy Bear, Teddy Bear

Read the poem. Then answer the questions.

Teddy Bear, Teddy Bear,
turn around.
Teddy Bear, Teddy Bear,
touch the ground.
Teddy Bear, Teddy Bear,
turn out the light.
Teddy Bear, Teddy Bear,
say good night.

Anonymous

1. Find the beat of the poem by clapping or jumping rope.

2. Circle all the **t**'s in the poem. Count them.

3. Draw a line under two words that rhyme.

Telling Time

Draw a line from each sentence to the clock that shows the correct time.

1. Tom wakes up at 8:00.

A.

2. Tasha eats lunch at 12:00.

B.

3. Ted rides his bike at 4:00.

C.

4. Teresa goes to bed at 7:30.

D.

 **Read About It**

Here's a book you might enjoy about time machines: *Alistair's Time Machine* by Marilyn Sadler.

66

Uu

Ursula the unicorn is under the umbrella.

Write each uppercase and
lowercase letter six times.

U

u

Draw something that begins with the letter **u**.
Write the word.

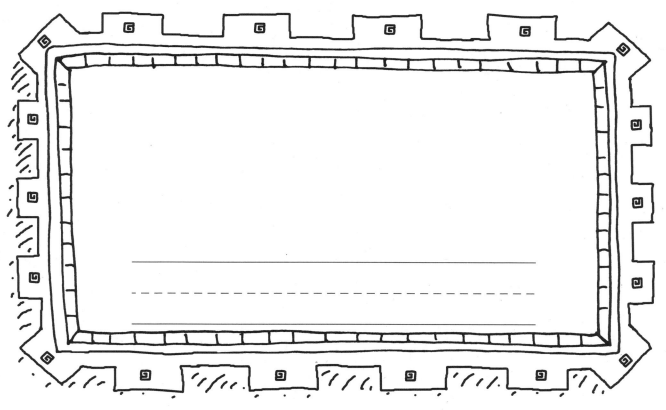

Under the Umbrella

Use the picture to fill in the missing vowels.

1. d ___ g   p___ g   t___ n   l___ g

2. f___ x   c___ t   h___ n   b___ d

3. h___ t   p___ t   n___ t   sh___ p

4. b___ ll   f___ sh   n___ st   l___ ck

United Under the Flag

Have an adult read this story about our flag to you. Do the activities and discussion questions together.

Flags have been used since ancient times. When you think of a flag, you might think of a colorful square of cloth. Did you know that some of the first flags were made from feathers and animal skins?

Flags are used as symbols for groups of people like countries or sports teams. Many people feel great pride for their country when they see their flag. This pride is called patriotism. An example of this is the pride of the athletes and spectators when their flag is raised during the Olympics.

Soon after becoming a new nation, Americans decided that they needed a flag. On June 14, 1777, the Continental Congress passed a law that said,

> "Resolved that the Flag of the United States be thirteen stripes alternate red and white: that the union be thirteen stars, white in a blue field, representing a new constellation."

Since the early days of our nation, we celebrate the birthday of our flag on June 14. This holiday is called Flag Day.

The first flag of the United States of America had only 13 stars, for our country's thirteen original colonies. As new states were added to our country, stars were added to our flag. Today we have fifty states, so there are fifty stars on our flag. However, there are still only thirteen stripes on our flag.

1. Here is a picture of the first American flag. The colors of that flag were the same as the colors of our flag today. Color the flag.

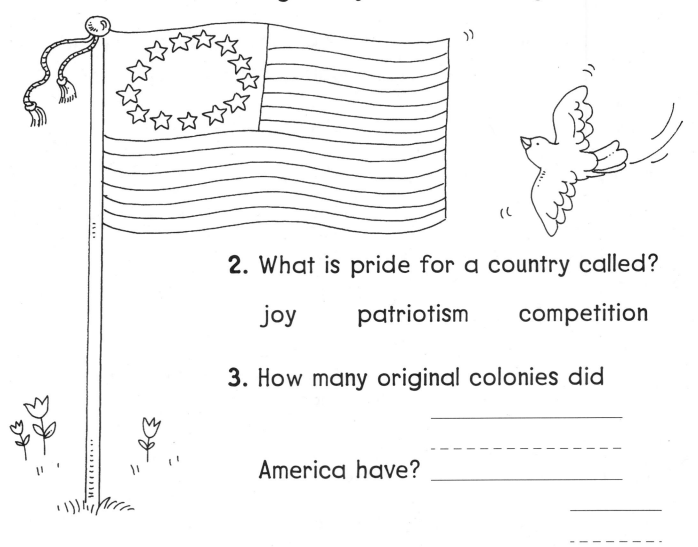

2. What is pride for a country called?

joy   patriotism   competition

3. How many original colonies did

_____

_ _ _ _ _ _ _ _ _ _ _ _

America have? _____

_ _ _ _ _

How many states does America have now?_____

4. Why is Flag Day on June 14?

_____

_ _

_____

V v

Victor the vulture plays the violin.

Write each uppercase and
lowercase letter six times.

V

v

Draw something that begins with the letter **v**.
Write the word.

Very Victor

Circle the things in the picture that start with the letter <u>v</u>.

Vowels

Long vowels say their name.
Print the missing long vowels.

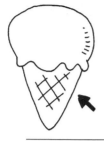

c _____ ne   sn _____ ke   tr _____ e

c _____ ne   r _____ pe   h _____ ve

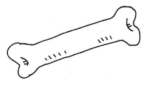

b _____ ne   c _____ ke   d _____ me

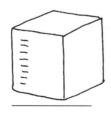
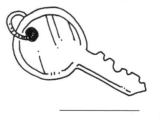

f _____ ve   c _____ be   k _____ y

Ww

Willie the worm is waving.

Write each uppercase and
lowercase letter six times.

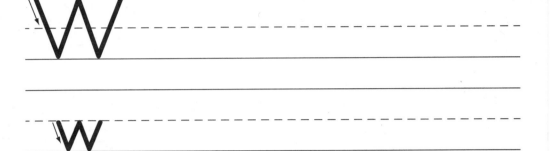

W

w

Draw something that begins with the letter <u>w</u>.
Write the word.

What Do You See?

Find something to describe. Look at it carefully.
Write about your object.

Object:
_____

Picture:
_____

Color:
_____

Texture:
_____

Size:
_____

Weight:
_____

Shape:
_____

What else do you notice?
_____

 **Read About It** Tana Hoban takes wonderful photographs of objects. One of her books is *Is It Rough? Is It Smooth? Is It Shiny?*

Wonderful World

There are seven continents in the world.
The United States of America is a country
on the continent of North America.

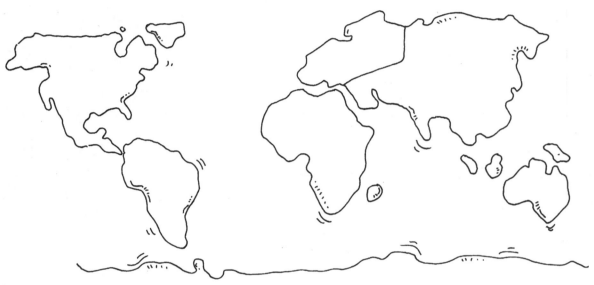

1. Color North America red.

2. Color South America blue.

3. Color Europe green.

4. Color Africa yellow.

5. Color Australia purple.

6. Color Antarctica brown.

7. Color Asia orange.

8. Draw an X on the continent where you live.

Xena the xylophone is on the X-ray.

Write each uppercase and
lowercase letter six times.

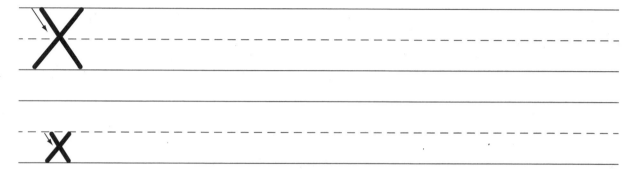

Draw something that begins with the letter **x**.
Write the word.

X It!

There are five children who are not following playground rules. Put an X on each of the five pictures.

Yy

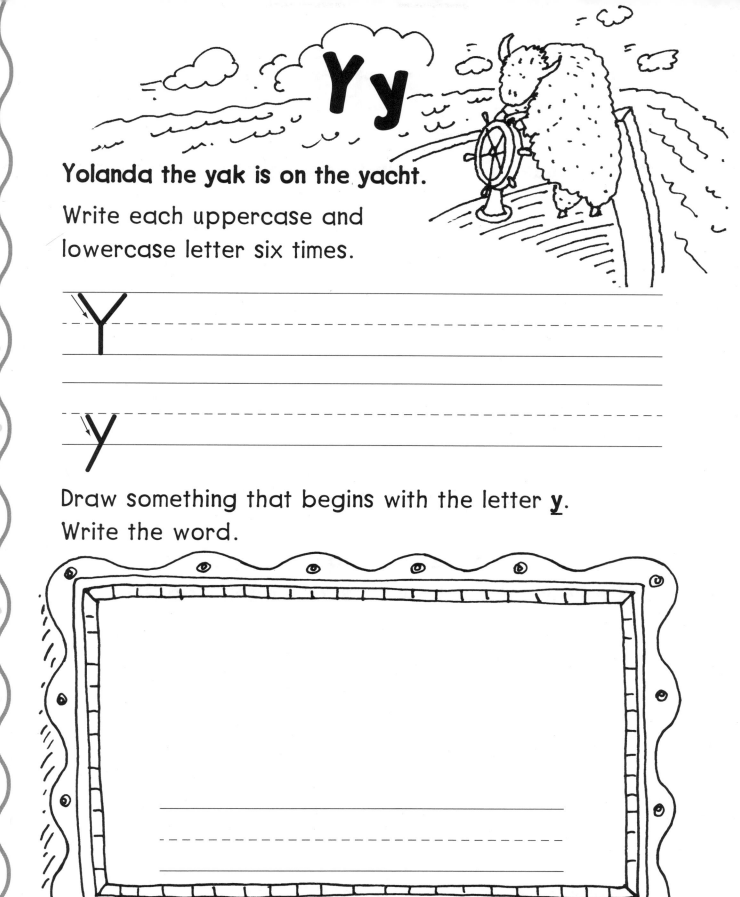

Yolanda the yak is on the yacht.

Write each uppercase and lowercase letter six times.

Y

y

Draw something that begins with the letter **y**.
Write the word.

Your Yardstick

Match these things to what they measure.

1.

   A. the time

2.

   B. how heavy

3.

   C. how hot or cold

4.

   D. how long or tall

Let's use small paper clips to measure length.
Write how many paper clips long each dog is.

5.    _____

6.    _____

7. Which dog is the longest? _____

Z z

Zack the zebra is in the zoo.

Write each uppercase and lowercase letter six times.

Z

z

Draw something that begins with the letter **z**. Write the word.

Zany Zoo

Answer the questions.

1. The zebra had 4 black stripes and 3 white stripes. How many stripes did the zebra have?

_____

- - - - - - - - - - - -

_____

2. Nick brought 4 pieces of bread to the zoo to feed the animals. He ate 2 pieces before he got there. How many pieces were left?

_____

- - - - - - - - - - - -

_____

3. When Emily got to the zoo, there were 8 school buses in the parking lot. Then, 4 buses drove away. How many buses were left?

_____

- - - - - - - - - - - -

_____

Zzzz...

Before you go to sleep tonight, write
a letter to a person who made you happy today.
Tell that person what made you so happy.

Dear _____ ,

_____

_____

_____

_____

_____

_____

_____

_____

_____

_____

_____

                                    _____

Love, _____

Book Section

The book section provides worksheets for three books. We hope you will read a lot more than three books this summer!

No More Water in the Tub! by Tedd Arnold

Hattie and the Fox by Mem Fox

The Napping House by Audrey Wood

No More Water in the Tub!

Read *No More Water in the Tub!* by Tedd Arnold, with an adult. Then talk about the questions.

1. Is this book about a real story? How do you know?

2. What started the trouble in the beginning of the book?

3. Does your mom or dad tell you things like "No more water in the tub"?

4. The last page is a huge surprise to the reader. What do we find out first when William thanks his brother Walter?

5. What do you think about the ending?

6. What was your favorite part?

7. Tedd Arnold uses rhyme in his story which helps the reader remember some silly facts. Do you remember what each character was riding?

Out went Mabel on the _____ .

Sue and Vern clung to a _____ .

Uncle Nash sat in the _____ .

Patty Fuzzle steered her _____ .

Little Dotty sailed the _____ .

Mr. Bellow rowed his _____ .

Read About It If you enjoyed this book, try
Tedd Arnold's *No Jumping on the Bed!*
Or, if you would like another imaginative
bathtub story, try *Effie's Bath*
by R. Thompson and E. Fernandes.

Hattie and the Fox

**Read *Hattie and the Fox*, by Mem Fox, with an adult.
Then talk about the questions.**

1. Did the story end the way you thought it would?

2. Why were Hattie and her friends so quiet
at the end of the book?

3. What did Hattie always say?

4. How did Hattie and her friends get rid
of the fox?

5. What other stories have a fox and a hen?

We know that whatever was in the bushes
had a nose, two eyes, two ears, a body,
four legs, and a tail. Mem Fox, the author,
told us that it was a fox. Draw a picture of
what else could have been in the bushes.

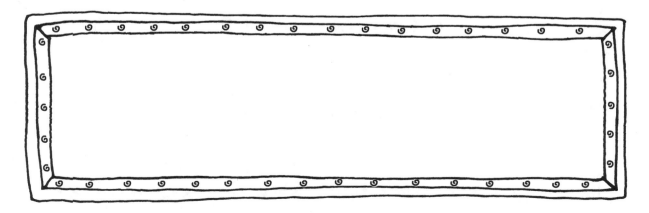

The Napping House

Read *The Napping House*, by Audrey Wood, with an adult. Then talk about the questions.

1. Were you surprised by the ending?

2. Leaf through the book from front to back and look at the pictures. What happens to the color of the pictures as you move toward the back of the book? Why?

3. Look at the pictures again. What clues to the story do you see?

4. This book uses wonderful words to describe the sleeping characters. What are some of the sleeping words?

5. What parts of the book could you read by yourself?

Draw a picture of your
favorite character in the book.

Answer Key

PAGE 6
1. 2 + 3 = 5
2. 1 + 4 = 5
3. 5 + 5 = 10
4. 3 + 4 = 7

PAGE 8
bananas, basket, beach ball,
bear, bed, Belle, bike,
bird, boat, book , boy,
bushes, butterfly

PAGE 10
1. B
2. D
3. E
4. A
5. C

PAGE 11
football, mailbox, rainbow, toothbrush, treehouse

PAGE 12
1. 12
2., 3. Answers will vary.

PAGE 13
3. 7
4. 30

PAGE 16
Sunday, Monday, Tuesday, Wednesday, Thursday, Friday,
Saturday

PAGE 18
1. ten, four, four, two
2. yellow, brown, red
3. ten
4. town

PAGE 19
1. 2
2. 2
3. 3
4. 4
5. 1

PAGE 21
1. b
2. a black shirt
3. white

PAGE 23
1. +   6. -
2. +   7. +
3. -   8. +
4. -   9. -
5. +   10. -

PAGE 26

1. sheep   5. Goldilocks
2. tuffet   6. grandmother
3. fat   7. three
4. soul   8. beanstalk

PAGE 27
X O X 0 X
X + X + X

PAGE 30
1. First and last sentences
2. west
3. south

PAGE 32
1. 1 inch
2. 2 inches
3. 3 inches

PAGE 34
1. Sam   4. hug
2. Pam   5. bug
3. ham   6. rug

PAGE 37
Circle king's crown, ball, pencil, can, glass.
Cross out keys, box, tub, chair, book.

PAGE 40
1. George Washington, answer varies
2. The country. They lived on a farm.
3. He taught himself.
4. He walked 3 miles
   to pay a woman 6 1/4¢.

PAGE 41
1. fifth
2. third
3. second
4. fourth
5. first

PAGE 43
1. red   6. 2
2. little   7. b
3. triangle   8. fat
4. 9   9. ten
5. five   10. b

PAGE 45
1. D
2. C
3. B
4. A

PAGE 47
1–8. Answers will vary.
9. 5
10. 5

89

11.	4	14.	6
12.	4	15.	6
13.	5	16.	6

PAGE 50
1. in
2. go
3. big
4. on
5. no

PAGE 51
Cross out: bat, swimsuit, hamburger, skates, bird

PAGE 53

1.
2.
3.
4.

PAGE 54
1. 9
2. shell, well
3. Suggested answers: bell, fell, sell, tell
4. Suggested answers: pig, peas, peach

PAGE 58
1. When you are waiting, time goes faster if you keep busy.
2. You can usually get something you want if you get there first.

PAGE 59
Suggested answers: rocket, pail, bug, jar, moon, bee

PAGE 60
1. belly, smelly
2. dish, fish
3. face, space
4. house, mouse
5. boat, coat
6. cake, rake
7. five, hive

PAGE 62
smell, taste
hear, see, touch

PAGE 65
1. 16
2. around/ground or light/night

PAGE 66
1. B
2. A
3. D
4. C

PAGE 68
1. dog, pig, ten, log
2. fox, cat, hen, bed
3. hat, pot, net, ship
4. bell, fish, nest, lock

PAGE 70
2. patriotism
3. 13, 50
4. It was the day the Continental Congress passed a law to make the first American flag.

PAGE 72
vacuum cleaner, vase, vegetables, vest, veterinarian, videotape, violets, violin, volcano, vulture, Victor, VCR

PAGE 73
1. cone, snake, tree
2. cane, rope, hive
3. bone, cake, dime
4. five, cube, key

PAGE 78
sliding backwards
standing on swing
cutting in line
pushing
running into street

PAGE 80
1. D
2. A
3. C
4. B
5. 1 paper clip
6. 2 paper clips
7. 6

PAGE 82
1. 7 stripes
2. 2 pieces
3. 4 buses

PAGES 85-86
1. not real; a bathtub would not fall that way
2. Walter twisted the handle of the tub to keep the water flowing in fast, but the handle broke off and the water kept running.
3. Answers will vary.
4. Walter was just telling William a story.
5, 6. Answers will vary.
7. table, fern, trash, puzzle, potty, cello

PAGE 87
1. Answers will vary.
2. They were so surprised, they were quiet.
3. Goodness, gracious, me!
4. Cow yelled "MOO!" to scare fox.
5. Suggested answers: Henny Penny, Rosie's Walk, Chicken Little

PAGE 88
1. Answers will vary.
2. They brighten and lighten as everyone wakes up.
3. The animals make their way around the room to the bed.
4. dozing, dreaming, snoring, slumbering, snoozing
5. Answers will vary.